TOILETRIVIA ™
WORLD HISTORY

The only trivia book that caters to your everyday bathroom needs

by Jeremy Klaff & Harry Klaff

This book might contain product names, trademarks, or registered trademarks. All trademarks in this book are property of their respective owners. If used, they are for non-biased use, and we do not encourage or discourage use of said product or service. Any term suspected of being a trademark will be properly capitalized.

Cover art by Stephanie Strack

About the Authors

Harry Klaff covered the NHL for *The Hockey News* and *Hockey Pictorial*, and reported for both the Associated Press and United Press International. He has written three books, *All Time Greatest Super Bowl*, *All Time Greatest Stanley Cup*, and *Computer Literacy and Use*.

Today, he is a retired Social Studies teacher from Brooklyn. Because he never went on a date in his adolescence, Harry had plenty of time to research useless facts and figures on everything ranging from history to pop culture. Moonlighting as a hockey scoreboard operator and baseball beer vendor, Harry had ample time to collect data.

Yet somehow, he got married. In 1977, Jeremy was born. Rather than being raised on a steady diet of carrots and peas, baby Jeremy was forced to learn facts from textbooks. His first word was "Uzbekistan." Throughout his childhood, Jeremy had a hard time making friends. When other kids wanted to play baseball, he wanted to instruct them about Henry VIII's six wives. After a failed career as a standup comic and broadcaster, in 2000 Jeremy fittingly became a Social Studies teacher. Today he brings trivia to the next generation.

Acknowledgements

We at Toiletrivia would like to thank all of the people who made this possible.

•The ancient cities of Harappa and Mohenjo Daro for engineering advances in plumbing.

•Sir John Harrington for inventing the modern flush toilet.

•Seth Wheeler for his patent of perforated toilet paper.

•Jeffrey Gunderson for inventing the plunger.

We would like to thank our families for suffering through nights of endless trivia.

We would also like to thank the friendly commuters at the Grand Central Station restroom facility for field testing these editions.

Introduction

Here at *Toiletrivia* we do extensive research on what you, the bathroom user, wish to see in your reading material. Sure, there are plenty of fine books out there to pass the time, but none of them cater to your competitive needs. That's why *Toiletrivia* is here to provide captivating trivia that allows you to interact with fellow bathroom users.

Each chapter allows you to keep score so you can evaluate your progress if you choose to go through the book multiple times. Or, you may wish to leave the book behind for others to play and keep score against you. Perhaps you just want to make it look like you are a genius, and leave a perfect scorecard for all to see. We hope you leave one in every bathroom of the house.

The rules of *Toiletrivia* are simple. Each chapter has 30 questions divided into three sections…One Roll, Two Rolls, or Three Rolls. The One Rolls are easiest and worth one point. Two Rolls are a bit harder and are worth two points. And of course, Three Rolls are the hardest, and are worth three points. You will tabulate your progress on the scorecard near the end of the book.

The questions we have selected are meant for dinner conversation, or impressing people you want to date. With few exceptions, our queries are geared for the uncomfortable situations that life throws at you, like when you have nothing in common with someone, and need to offer some clever banter. We hope that the facts you learn in the restroom make it easier to meet your future in-laws, or deal with that hairdresser who just won't stop talking to you.

Remember, *Toiletrivia* is a game. No joysticks, no computer keyboards…just you, your toilet, and a pen; the way nature intended it. So good luck. We hope you are triumphant.

DIRECTIONS

Each set of questions has an answer sheet opposite it. Write your answers in the first available column to the right. When you are done with a set of 10 questions, *fold* your answer column underneath so the next restroom user doesn't see your answers. *Special note to restroom users 2 and 3: No cheating! And the previous person's answers might be wrong!*

Then check your responses with the answer key in the back of the book. Mark your right answers with a check, and your wrong answers with an "x." Then go to the scorecard on pages 98-100 and tabulate your results. These totals will be the standard for other users to compare.

Be sure to look online for other Toiletrivia titles
Visit us at www.toiletrivia.com

Table of Contents

Rulers

 ## One Roll

Flip to pg. 68 for answers

1. What leader of the Aztecs was conquered by Hernando Cortes? He would get his revenge centuries later when tourists drank Mexican water.

2. Which famed female leader of Israel previously lived in Wisconsin?

3. What was the First Czar of All of Russia more commonly known as? Did we mention that he killed his own son?

4. Which inspiring leader walked 240 miles to the Indian Ocean to collect salt?

5. Which leader made millions of followers carry around a little red book of his quotations?

6. Which woman received visions from God to liberate France from England in the Hundred Years' War?

7. Which undefeated military leader who amassed an extensive empire was also tutored by Aristotle?

8. Which Hapsburg was assassinated on June 28th, 1914 to trigger WWI?

9. Who is the most powerful Frenchman to ever be born in Corsica?

10. Which ancient Babylonian king demanded an "eye for an eye"?

Answer Sheet

Rulers
1 Roll

Name_____

Answer Sheet

Rulers
1 Roll

Name_____

Answer Sheet

Rulers
1 Roll

Name_____

1.	1.	1.
2.	2.	2.
3.	3.	3.
4.	4.	4.
5.	5.	5.
6.	6.	6.
7.	7.	7.
8.	8.	8.
9.	9.	9.
10.	10.	10.

After you have filled out the sheet, fold your column underneath along the dashed line so the next restroom user won't see your answers. ***The first player uses the far right column.***

Notes:

Notes:

Notes:

Rulers

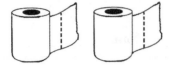

Two Rolls

Flip to pg. 69 for answers

1. Nicknamed "The Sun King," he was the monarch of France who expanded and renovated the Palace of Versailles.

2. Founder of the Mongol Empire, his name at birth was Temujin.

3. Who led a revolution in 1917, yet his body is still viewable on Earth?

4. For whom was the Great Pyramid of Giza supposed to be the final resting place for?

5. Infamously accused of saying, "Let them eat cake," which famous Queen's reported last words were an apology for stepping on the executioner's foot?

6. Who coined the term, "Iron Curtain," when referring to the USSR's satellites after WWII? He also delivered the "Finest Hour" speech.

7. Which leader of Rome had a gigantic wall built to mark the northernmost border of the Roman Empire?

8. Which American President died shortly after the Yalta Conference?

9. Known as "The Liberator," which revolutionary helped rid South America of Spanish rule?

10. Which Fascist Spanish leader is "still dead" according to *Saturday Night Live*?

Answer Sheet

Rulers
2 Rolls

Name_____

Answer Sheet

Rulers
2 Rolls

Name_____

Answer Sheet

Rulers
2 Rolls

Name_____

1.	1.	1.
2.	2.	2.
3.	3.	3.
4.	4.	4.
5.	5.	5.
6.	6.	6.
7.	7.	7.
8.	8.	8.
9.	9.	9.
10.	10.	10.

After you have filled out the sheet, fold your column underneath along the dashed line so the next restroom user won't see your answers. *The first player uses the far right column.*

Notes:

Notes:

Notes:

Rulers

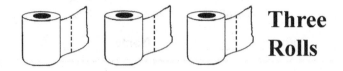

Three Rolls

Flip to pg. 70 for answers

1. Which emperor of the Byzantine Empire created his own "Code" of laws?

2. Who was the first US President to die in office?

3. What was Peter the Great's family name?

4. Which leader of the Mughal Empire created the Taj Mahal in honor of his wife?

5. Who do Egyptologists accept to be the longest reigning, and strongest female pharaoh of ancient Egypt?

6. Who unified Germany with "Blood and Iron"?

7. Nicknamed "the first citizen of Athens," this statesman and military general gained power during the Golden Age of Athens.

8. Which Prussian leader, a proponent of the arts, would also be a thorn in the side of Maria Theresa in Silesia?

9. Just before the outbreak of WWII, which British Prime Minister proclaimed that the Munich Conference would give Europe "Peace in Our Time"?

10. Despite being exiled from his native Ethiopia after an Italian conquest in 1935, this Emperor later returned to rule his native country until 1974.

Answer Sheet   Answer Sheet   Answer Sheet

Rulers   **Rulers**   **Rulers**
3 Rolls   **3 Rolls**   **3 Rolls**

Name_____ Name_____ Name_____

1.	1.	1.
2.	2.	2.
3.	3.	3.
4.	4.	4.
5.	5.	5.
6.	6.	6.
7.	7.	7.
8.	8.	8.
9.	9.	9.
10.	10.	10.

After you have filled out the sheet, fold your column underneath along the dashed line so the next restroom user won't see your answers. ***The first player uses the far right column.***

Notes: *Notes:*   *Notes:*

Wars

One Roll

Flip to pg. 71 for answers

1. Ironically, it had rained just before Napoleon met his final defeat here.

2. What "day," the largest invasion of WWII, had an estimated 160,000 Allied troops, 5,000 ships, and 13,000 aircraft?

3. If one does the math correctly, 1337-1457 should be called the 120 Years War between England and France, instead of this.

4. Which American war had more deaths and casualties than all other American wars combined?

5. Which 1962 international crisis involving John F. Kennedy, Nikita Khrushchev, and Fidel Castro, lasted 13 October days before ending peacefully?

6. What group of conflicts began when Pope Urban II called for a war in the Holy Land?

7. What was nicknamed, "The Great War," until receiving a new name in 1939?

8. Which leader of the Free French Forces of WWII currently has an airport in France named for him?

9. What was the name of the plane that dropped the atomic bomb on Hiroshima?

10. What did Albert Einstein say that World War IV would be fought with?

Answer Sheet | # Answer Sheet | # Answer Sheet

<table>
<tr><td>Wars
1 Roll</td><td>Wars
1 Roll</td><td>Wars
1 Roll</td></tr>
</table>

Name_____ Name_____ Name_____

1.	1.	1.
2.	2.	2.
3.	3.	3.
4.	4.	4.
5.	5.	5.
6.	6.	6.
7.	7.	7.
8.	8.	8.
9.	9.	9.
10.	10.	10.

After you have filled out the sheet, fold your column underneath along the dashed line so the next restroom user won't see your answers. ***The first player uses the far right column.***

Notes: *Notes:*   *Notes:*

Wars

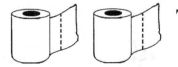

Two Rolls

Flip to pg. 72 for answers

1. Meaning "tiger," but inferring "charge," or "attack," what phrase was screamed by Japanese pilots at Pearl Harbor?

2. Who commanded a sneak attack on the Romans by trekking on elephants across the Alps in the Second Punic War?

3. What city fell to Vietnamese Communists in 1954?

4. Who went on a 6,000 mile-long march to flee the Nationalists in the Chinese Civil War?

5. What cruise liner was sunk on May 7, 1915 by a German U-boat, thereby moving the United States closer to entering WWI?

6. Which ancient war (or wars) in the Fifth Century BC, engulfed the Greek peninsula as a quasi-civil war between city-states?

7. What series of British civil wars were named for a flower?

8. What did British-American colonists call the Seven Years' War?

9. Which parallel did North Korea cross to invade South Korea in 1950?

10. Who was the leader of the Red Army during the Russian Civil War?

Answer Sheet | Answer Sheet | Answer Sheet

Wars
2 Rolls

Wars
2 Rolls

Wars
2 Rolls

Name_____ Name_____ Name_____

1.	1.	1.
2.	2.	2.
3.	3.	3.
4.	4.	4.
5.	5.	5.
6.	6.	6.
7.	7.	7.
8.	8.	8.
9.	9.	9.
10.	10.	10.

After you have filled out the sheet, fold your column underneath along the dashed line so the next restroom user won't see your answers. ***The first player uses the far right column.***

Notes: | *Notes:* | *Notes:*

Wars

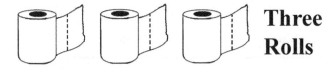 **Three Rolls**

Flip to pg. 73 for answers

1. What war was partially ignited when three Catholics were "defenestrated" (thrown out of a window) from Prague Castle in 1618?

2. Which WWII battle caused the most American casualties?

3. Florence Nightingale was one of history's most famous nurses. In what war was she sent by Britain to help treat cholera in Turkey?

4. Which 1688 bloodless overthrow of King James II ended with William and Mary taking the English throne?

5. Who assassinated Archduke Franz Ferdinand to trigger the chain reaction that ignited WWI?

6. What mutiny in India began in 1857 when Hindu and Muslim soldiers heard they were being given meat-flavored gunpowder pouches to bite open?

7. What is the only international war (1739-1748) to ever be named for a person's body part?

8. Within five, how many Nazis were charged with crimes at the Nuremberg Trials?

9. Which war's peace conference was held in Portsmouth, New Hampshire, becoming the first foreign war ever to be resolved in the United States?

10. Which series of wars allowed Britain to become fortified in the Union of South Africa?

Answer Sheet | Answer Sheet | Answer Sheet

Wars 3 Rolls	Wars 3 Rolls	Wars 3 Rolls
Name_____	Name_____	Name_____
1.	1.	1.
2.	2.	2.
3.	3.	3.
4.	4.	4.
5.	5.	5.
6.	6.	6.
7.	7.	7.
8.	8.	8.
9.	9.	9.
10.	10.	10.

After you have filled out the sheet, fold your column underneath along the dashed line so the next restroom user won't see your answers. ***The first player uses the far right column.***

Notes: | *Notes:* | *Notes:*

World Landmarks

 One Roll

Flip to pg. 74 for answers

1. What Ming structure encompassing 3,700-4,000 miles was constructed to keep out foreign invaders from the North?

2. What is the largest of the Ancient Wonders of the World?

3. What famed London church is the final resting place of Charles Darwin? It has also been the site for royal weddings, including the 2011 marriage of Prince William and Catherine Middleton.

4. Where in France are the beaches of D-Day?

5. At what palace was the treaty to end WWI signed?

6. One of the New Seven Wonders of the World, in what city would one find the approximately 130-foot tall Christ the Redeemer statue?

7. What is the heaviest calendar on Salisbury Plain?

8. What famous French prison was stormed on July 14, 1789?

9. What is the remaining part of the Second Temple built by Herod the Great called today? Hundreds visit every day to pray.

10. What gets a new coat of paint every seven years, and is constructed of 18,038 iron modular components? Oh, by the way, it was believed to be an eyesore of the Parisian skyline when it opened in 1889.

Answer Sheet | Answer Sheet | Answer Sheet

World Landmarks
1 Roll

World Landmarks
1 Roll

World Landmarks
1 Roll

Name_____ Name_____ Name_____

1.	1.	1.
2.	2.	2.
3.	3.	3.
4.	4.	4.
5.	5.	5.
6.	6.	6.
7.	7.	7.
8.	8.	8.
9.	9.	9.
10.	10.	10.

After you have filled out the sheet, fold your column underneath along the dashed line so the next restroom user won't see your answers. *The first player uses the far right column.*

Notes: | *Notes:* | *Notes:*

World Landmarks

Two Rolls

Flip to pg. 75 for answers

1. Which lost Peruvian city was rediscovered by Hiram Bingham in 1911?

2. What famous American obelisk took about 40 years to complete?

3. Where are the remains of the USS *Arizona*?

4. What famous Mayan city in the Yucatán is home to the Temple of Kukulkan, which was renamed El Castillo (the castle) by the Spanish?

5. What is the largest enclosed square in Beijing?

6. What city is home to the Taj Mahal?

7. Which god or goddess is the Parthenon dedicated to?

8. Where does legend have Galileo dropping items from approximately 184 feet in the air to test his theories?

9. Where are the famous South American ancient "lines" that depict animal patterns in the sand?

10. What is the name of the brightly colored cathedral in the landscape of the Kremlin and Red Square?

Answer Sheet

World Landmarks
2 Rolls

Name_____

Answer Sheet

World Landmarks
2 Rolls

Name_____

Answer Sheet

World Landmarks
2 Rolls

Name_____

1.	1.	1.
2.	2.	2.
3.	3.	3.
4.	4.	4.
5.	5.	5.
6.	6.	6.
7.	7.	7.
8.	8.	8.
9.	9.	9.
10.	10.	10.

After you have filled out the sheet, fold your column underneath along the dashed line so the next restroom user won't see your answers. *The first player uses the far right column.*

Notes: *Notes:* *Notes:*

World Landmarks

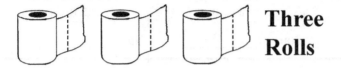

Three Rolls

Flip to pg. 76 for answers

1. The Statue of Liberty has a twin. Where does she live?

2. In what famous room was the treaty that ended WWI signed?

3. On what island would one find the Temple of Knossos?

4. What city that houses the Dutch Parliament calls itself, "The International City of Peace and Justice"?

5. What famous temple in the Cambodian jungle is the largest religious structure in the world?

6. What "city" in China has 9,999 rooms?

7. What famous Byzantine Church was built under the reign of Justinian I in Byzantium?

8. What is the famous city carved in rock by the Nabateans in modern day Jordan?

9. Where did people from kings to commoners visit the most famous oracle of ancient Greece?

10. Begun in 1882, what famous Antoni Gaudi project in Barcelona is still not completed?

Answer Sheet   Answer Sheet   Answer

World Landmarks   World Landmarks   World Landmarks
3 Rolls   3 Rolls   3 Rolls

Name_____ Name_____ Name_____

1.	1.	1.
2.	2.	2.
3.	3.	3.
4.	4.	4.
5.	5.	5.
6.	6.	6.
7.	7.	7.
8.	8.	8.
9.	9.	9.
10.	10.	10.

After you have filled out the sheet, fold your column underneath along the dashed line so the next restroom user won't see your answers. ***The first player uses the far right column.***

Notes: *Notes:*   *Notes:*

History Before 1800

 One Roll

Flip to pg. 77 for answers

1. "Molasses to Rum to Slaves" completes which infamous international trade route?

2. Where was gunpowder first used?

3. *Yersinia Pestis* is the bacteria associated with what devastating illness that spread through Europe and Asia around 1350?

4. What Norse explorer is thought to have landed in the New World hundreds of years before Columbus?

5. If the ancient Sumerians wrote in cuneiform, then what did the ancient Egyptians write in?

6. Which British woman was referred to as "The Virgin Queen?"

7. What contraption used to decapitate people during the French Revolution was defended by its inventor to be a humane form of execution?

8. What word was given to those who protested the Catholic Church in the 16th Century?

9. What did Emperor Qin Shi Huang surround his tomb with?

10. What Balkan empire, first founded by Osman I, later became the "Sick Man of Europe" before WWI?

Answer Sheet | # Answer Sheet | # Answer Sheet

History Before 1800
1 Roll

History Before 1800
1 Roll

History Before 1800
1 Roll

Name_____ Name_____ Name_____

1.	1.	1.
2.	2.	2.
3.	3.	3.
4.	4.	4.
5.	5.	5.
6.	6.	6.
7.	7.	7.
8.	8.	8.
9.	9.	9.
10.	10.	10.

After you have filled out the sheet, fold your column underneath along the dashed line so the next restroom user won't see your answers. ***The first player uses the far right column.***

Notes: | *Notes:* | *Notes:*

History Before 1800

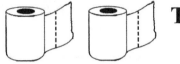

Two Rolls

Flip to pg. 78 for answers

1. What volcano erupted in 79 AD covering the area around modern day Naples in volcanic ash?

2. Which Russian monarch was rumored to be killed in a sexual encounter with a horse?

3. What trade routes brought goods from Asia to Rome around 400 AD?

4. In 1799 Napoleon suddenly seized power in France. What is the French term for this "blow of state?"

5. What was Shakespeare's theater in England called? In 1613 it burned to the ground during a production of *Henry VIII* when a cannon set the stage on fire.

6. During the French Revolution, on what type of sports playing surface did peasants take an oath to make a new Constitution?

7. What ancient warrior adhered to the bushido code?

8. Who was the wise son of David that built the First Temple in Jerusalem?

9. According to myth, which twins founded Rome?

10. Which act that was passed during the reign of Charles II made it illegal to imprison someone without a trial? Today, the President of the United States can suspend this right "when in cases of rebellion or invasion the public safety may require it."

Answer Sheet

History Before 1800
2 Rolls

Name_____

1.
2.
3.
4.
5.
6.
7.
8.
9.
10.

Answer Sheet

History Before 1800
2 Rolls

Name_____

1.
2.
3.
4.
5.
6.
7.
8.
9.
10.

Answer Sheet

History Before 1800
2 Rolls

Name_____

1.
2.
3.
4.
5.
6.
7.
8.
9.
10.

After you have filled out the sheet, fold your column underneath along the dashed line so the next restroom user won't see your answers. *The first player uses the far right column.*

Notes:

Notes:

Notes:

History Before 1800

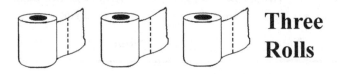

Three Rolls

Flip to pg. 79 for answers

1. How many wives did Henry VIII have?

2. Which Babylonian King who conquered Jerusalem has his name used today to measure wine? 14 letters.

3. What epic Sumerian poem is one of the earliest works of literature written anywhere in the world? The story details the heroic adventures of a king looking for immortality. OK, it starts with the letter G.

4. What is the collection of 1648 peace treaties that ended the Thirty Years' War called?

5. What Cervantes novel finds the protagonist attacking windmills he believes to be giants?

6. What real life Transylvanian was the inspiration behind the story of *Dracula*?

7. Who was the pharaoh of Egypt who "wouldn't let Moses' people go"?

8. Which king was beheaded in 1649 when Oliver Cromwell took over after the English Civil War?

9. What seafaring ancient people created an alphabet that would be adopted by the Greeks, and eventually become the alphabet we use today?

10. Which ancient Sumerian city's name would only get you two points in Scrabble?

Answer Sheet

History Before 1800
3 Rolls

Name_____

Answer Sheet

History Before 1800
3 Rolls

Name_____

Answer Sheet

History Before 1800
3 Rolls

Name_____

1.	1.	1.
2.	2.	2.
3.	3.	3.
4.	4.	4.
5.	5.	5.
6.	6.	6.
7.	7.	7.
8.	8.	8.
9.	9.	9.
10.	10.	10.

After you have filled out the sheet, fold your column underneath along the dashed line so the next restroom user won't see your answers. *The first player uses the far right column.*

Notes:

Notes:

Notes:

Popular Culture

Flip to pg. 80 for answers

One Roll

1. One of the famous "Three Tenors," he had key roles in the operas *La Bohème, L'Elisir,* and *Madame Butterfly,* and was also an expert in equestrian jumping.

2. Which Dickens classic details an orphan working in terrible conditions during the Industrial Revolution? *Please sir, I want some more.*

3. What Spanish dance that sounds like the name of a pink bird in Florida, has spread to Latin America to become even more popular?

4. Which famed impressionist painter handed over his left ear to a prostitute? Whether or not he cut if off himself is still open to debate.

5. Where are movies in India made? "Hooray for...

6. Which famed German composer might have lost his hearing because he had the habit of immersing his head in cold water before performing?

7. What popular rock group of the "British Invasion" was formed in Liverpool in 1960?

8. Jørn Utzon designed which iconic Australian performing arts center that seems to float on the water?

9. Which ancient structure where gladiators fought lions was used before and during WWII as a center for Fascist rallies?

10. Which American sport, invented by a Canadian, was originally intended to keep a bunch of rowdy kids under control in gym class?

Answer Sheet
Popular Culture
1 Roll

Name_____

Answer Sheet
Popular Culture
1 Roll

Name_____

Answer Sheet
Popular Culture
1 Roll

Name_____

1.	1.	1.
2.	2.	2.
3.	3.	3.
4.	4.	4.
5.	5.	5.
6.	6.	6.
7.	7.	7.
8.	8.	8.
9.	9.	9.
10.	10.	10.

After you have filled out the sheet, fold your column underneath along the dashed line so the next restroom user won't see your answers. *The first player uses the far right column.*

Notes: *Notes:*   *Notes:*

Popular Culture

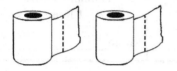 **Two Rolls**

Flip to pg. 81 for answers

1. In what city would you find the Prostitution Information Center?

2. What city hosts the most popular Running of the Bulls?

3. What historic Japanese poem is divided into three lines of 5, 7, and 5 syllables each?

4. In what Italian city was the word "pizza" used for the first time to describe flatbreads with toppings?

5. Who is the famous Dutch painter whose detailed works include *The Night Watch,* and *The Syndics of the Clothmakers' Guild*?

6. What does CBS stand for?

7. Known for their psychedelic rock style, which English band sang about *The Dark Side of the Moon*?

8. Where was the first modern-day Olympics held in 1896?

9. What Sophocles tragedy tells the story of a king who accidentally falls in love with his mother?

10. What food is historically eaten at Wimbledon matches?

Answer Sheet   Answer Sheet   Answer Sheet

Popular Culture
2 Rolls

Popular Culture
2 Rolls

Popular Culture
2 Rolls

Name_____ Name_____ Name_____

1.	1.	1.
2.	2.	2.
3.	3.	3.
4.	4.	4.
5.	5.	5.
6.	6.	6.
7.	7.	7.
8.	8.	8.
9.	9.	9.
10.	10.	10.

After you have filled out the sheet, fold your column underneath along the dashed line so the next restroom user won't see your answers. ***The first player uses the far right column.***

Notes: *Notes:*   *Notes:*

Popular Culture

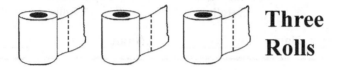

Three Rolls

Flip to pg. 82 for answers

1. Since 1975, what famous street has the Tour de France finished on?

2. What is the name of the Japanese theater activity that involves heavy makeup and cross-dressing?

3. What do people do with tomatoes every year in the village of Buñol, Spain?

4. Which Shakespearean character is referred to as "The Moor"?

5. Where in Austria do horses, still to this day, learn how to dance?

6. Which Peruvian delicacy is composed of fresh raw fish and citrus juices?

7. Who sculpted *The Thinker*?

8. What meeting center of Ancient Rome was used for chariot races and religious festivals? Probably didn't have trapeze acts, though.

9. What were the musicians in Middle Age castles known as?

10. Since 2000, what country has had the highest per capita beer consumption rate in the world?

Answer Sheet

Popular Culture
3 Rolls

Name_____

Answer Sheet

Popular Culture
3 Rolls

Name_____

Answer Sheet

Popular Culture
3 Rolls

Name_____

1.	1.	1.
2.	2.	2.
3.	3.	3.
4.	4.	4.
5.	5.	5.
6.	6.	6.
7.	7.	7.
8.	8.	8.
9.	9.	9.
10.	10.	10.

After you have filled out the sheet, fold your column underneath along the dashed line so the next restroom user won't see your answers. ***The first player uses the far right column.***

Notes: *Notes:*   *Notes:*

Religion and Philosophy

One Roll

Flip to pg. 83 for answers

1. Where did Moses receive the Ten Commandments?

2. What religion would find it bad karma not to know what karma means?

3. What building releases smoke when a new Pope is crowned at the Vatican?

4. Which religion has the Five Pillars?

5. Who wrote *The Republic*?

6. What is the largest practicing religion in the world?

7. Who wrote the 95 Theses?

8. What is the Holiest book of Islam?

9. What book in the Old Testament comes after Genesis?

10. Who was father of the gods of Ancient Greece?

Answer Sheet

Religion and Philosophy
1 Roll

Name_____

1.	1.	1.
2.	2.	2.
3.	3.	3.
4.	4.	4.
5.	5.	5.
6.	6.	6.
7.	7.	7.
8.	8.	8.
9.	9.	9.
10.	10.	10.

Answer Sheet

Religion and Philosophy
1 Roll

Name_____

Answer Sheet

Religion and Philosophy
1 Roll

Name_____

After you have filled out the sheet, fold your column underneath along the dashed line so the next restroom user won't see your answers. ***The first player uses the far right column.***

Notes:

Notes:

Notes:

Religion and Philosophy

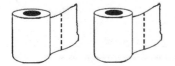 ## Two Rolls

Flip to pg. 84 for answers

1. What cube-shaped building in Mecca is the holiest site of Islam?

2. What ancient set of spiritual beliefs from Japan is still practiced today?

3. In what spiritual book of Hinduism would one find the main character Krishna?

4. What is the largest sect of Christianity?

5. What was the first of the ten plagues?

6. Who wrote the Analects?

7. What word in Buddhism means to release from selfishness, suffering, and materialism? It's also the name of a popular 1990s rock band. It's not Pearl Jam.

8. What type of religion did Joseph Stalin preach in the Soviet Union?

9. What funerary text was written on papyrus?

10. What is the hajj?

Answer Sheet

Religion and Philosophy
2 Rolls

Name_____

Answer Sheet

Religion and Philosophy
2 Rolls

Name_____

Answer Sheet

Religion and Philosophy
2 Rolls

Name_____

1.	1.	1.
2.	2.	2.
3.	3.	3.
4.	4.	4.
5.	5.	5.
6.	6.	6.
7.	7.	7.
8.	8.	8.
9.	9.	9.
10.	10.	10.

After you have filled out the sheet, fold your column underneath along the dashed line so the next restroom user won't see your answers. ***The first player uses the far right column.***

Notes:

Notes:

Notes:

Religion and Philosophy

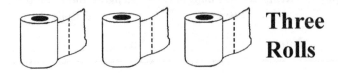

Three Rolls

Flip to pg. 85 for answers

1. What was Buddha's name?

2. In Hinduism, who is the protector, or pre-server?

3. Written by Laozi (Lao Tzu), what is the most influential text of Daoism?

4. What figure in the Myth of Osiris was the ancient Egyptian goddess of fertility?

5. The Egyptians called him Ra. The Incas called him Inti, and the Aztecs called him Huitzilopochtli. What was he the god of?

6. What religion's sects include Mahayana and Theravada?

7. Who was the Roman god of the underworld? We don't mean the Disney character.

8. What spiritual and mystical movement contains the texts of the Sefer Yetzirah, and the Zohar?

9. What religion believes that everything has a soul, and will not harm anything living? Some practicing people even wear masks to prevent them from accidentally eating an insect.

10. What Chinese book gave prophecies based on coin tosses?

Answer Sheet

Religion and Philosophy
3 Rolls

Name_____

Answer Sheet

Religion and Philosophy
3 Rolls

Name_____

Answer Sheet

Religion and Philosophy
3 Rolls

Name_____

1.	1.	1.
2.	2.	2.
3.	3.	3.
4.	4.	4.
5.	5.	5.
6.	6.	6.
7.	7.	7.
8.	8.	8.
9.	9.	9.
10.	10.	10.

After you have filled out the sheet, fold your column underneath along the dashed line so the next restroom user won't see your answers. *The first player uses the far right column.*

Notes:

Notes:

Notes:

Dates (Get within 5 years either way)

 One Roll

Flip to pg. 86 for answers

1. Pearl Harbor

2. The Bastille is stormed

3. Columbus sails the ocean blue

4. Man steps on the moon

5. Osama bin Laden killed by Navy Seals

6. Treaty of Versailles ending WWI

7. US Stock Market crash before the Great Depression

8. Bolshevik Revolution

9. D-Day

10. Year the Mayans predicted the world would end

Answer Sheet　Answer Sheet　Answ

Dates
1 Roll

Dates
1 Roll

Name_____ Name_____ Name_____

1.	1.	1.
2.	2.	2.
3.	3.	3.
4.	4.	4.
5.	5.	5.
6.	6.	6.
7.	7.	7.
8.	8.	8.
9.	9.	9.
10.	10.	10.

After you have filled out the sheet, fold your column underneath along the dashed line so the next restroom user won't see your answers. ***The first player uses the far right column.***

Notes:　*Notes:*　*Notes:*

ates (Get within 5 years either way)

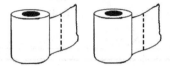

Two Rolls

Flip to pg. 87 for answers

1. Battle of Hastings (that's the one with William the Conqueror)

2. Spanish Armada loses to England

3. Berlin Wall comes down

4. Indian Independence

5. Ides of March when Caesar was killed

6. Prince Charles marries Princess Diana

7. People's Republic of China declared in Tiananmen Square

8. Six Day War

9. UN is formed

10. Magna Carta is signed

Answer Sheet | Answer Sheet | Answer Sheet

Answer Sheet Answer Sheet

Dates
2 Rolls

Dates
2 Rolls

Dates
2 Rolls

Name_____ Name_____ Name_____

1.	1.	1.
2.	2.	2.
3.	3.	3.
4.	4.	4.
5.	5.	5.
6.	6.	6.
7.	7.	7.
8.	8.	8.
9.	9.	9.
10.	10.	10.

After you have filled out the sheet, fold your column underneath along the dashed line so the next restroom user won't see your answers. *The first player uses the far right column.*

Notes: *Notes:*   *Notes:*

Dates (Get within 5 years either way)

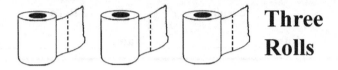 **Three Rolls**

Flip to pg. 88 for answers

1. Start of the Crimean War

2. Napoleon crowns himself Emperor

3. Fall of Rome

4. Socrates drinks poison

5. Congress of Vienna

6. Franco-Prussian War

7. Charlemagne crowned Holy Roman Emperor

8. Louisiana Purchase

9. *Communist Manifesto* is published

10. Boxer Rebellion

Answer Sheet | Answer Sheet | Answer Sheet

Dates
3 Rolls

Dates
3 Rolls

Dates
3 Rolls

Name_____ Name_____ Name_____

1.	1.	1.
2.	2.	2.
3.	3.	3.
4.	4.	4.
5.	5.	5.
6.	6.	6.
7.	7.	7.
8.	8.	8.
9.	9.	9.
10.	10.	10.

After you have filled out the sheet, fold your column underneath along the dashed line so the next restroom user won't see your answers. *The first player uses the far right column.*

Notes: | *Notes:* | *Notes:*

Historical People

Flip to pg. 89 for answers

 One Roll

1. Who wrote *The Iliad* and *The Odyssey*?

2. Who painted the *Mona Lisa*?

3. Who served 27 years in a South African prison before the end of apartheid?

4. Who painted the ceiling of the Sistine Chapel?

5. What were the Wright Brothers' first names?

6. Which famed European traveler to China is not mentioned in Chinese books of the time? Maybe no one saw him playing in the pool.

7. Which famous female humanitarian of Calcutta was beatified by Pope John Paul II a few years after her death in 1997?

8. Which psychologist who investigated the unconscious mind, sexual repression, and dreams, had his office turned into a modern day museum in Vienna?

9. Sadly, this brilliant woman died from radiation poisoning that resulted from her research.

10. In 1927, who flew solo from New York to Paris in 33½ hours?

Answer Sheet

Historical People
1 Roll

Name_____

Answer Sheet

Historical People
1 Roll

Name_____

Answer Sheet

Historical People
1 Roll

Name_____

1.	1.	1.
2.	2.	2.
3.	3.	3.
4.	4.	4.
5.	5.	5.
6.	6.	6.
7.	7.	7.
8.	8.	8.
9.	9.	9.
10.	10.	10.

After you have filled out the sheet, fold your column underneath along the dashed line so the next restroom user won't see your answers. *The first player uses the far right column.*

Notes: *Notes:*   *Notes:*

Historical People

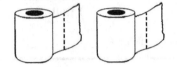

Two Rolls

Flip to pg. 90 for answers

1. Who sculpted the statue of *David*?

2. Who painted *The School of Athens*?

3. Along with Karl Marx, who also wrote *The Communist Manifesto*?

4. Whose *The Origin of Species* was perhaps the most controversial work ever written?

5. What did Johan Gutenberg invent?

6. Who was the first explorer to circumnavigate the Earth?

7. Who discovered the vaccine for polio?

8. Which young Egyptian ruler became a lot more famous when his tomb was found completely intact in 1922?

9. To whom do most give credit for the invention of the first practical commercially used steamboat? He is buried next to another very famous American.

10. Who wrote the gothic novel *Frankenstein*?

Answer Sheet

Historical People
2 Rolls

Name_____

1.
2.
3.
4.
5.
6.
7.
8.
9.
10.

Answer Sheet

Historical People
2 Rolls

Name_____

1.
2.
3.
4.
5.
6.
7.
8.
9.
10.

Answer Sheet

Historical People
2 Rolls

Name_____

1.
2.
3.
4.
5.
6.
7.
8.
9.
10.

After you have filled out the sheet, fold your column underneath along the dashed line so the next restroom user won't see your answers. *The first player uses the far right column.*

Notes: *Notes:*   *Notes:*

Historical People

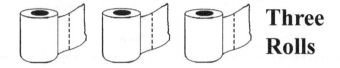

Three Rolls

Flip to pg. 91 for answers

1. What Russian was the pioneer of psychological classical conditioning? Some thought his career went to the dogs.

2. What was François Marie Arouet better known as?

3. Which leader of the Wars of Scottish Independence was played by Mel Gibson in *Braveheart*?

4. Which Austrian prince and foreign minister was the most influential diplomat at the Congress of Vienna?

5. What book did Sun Tzu write in which he detailed the importance of knowing one's enemy? Business people still read this ancient text today to get an edge.

6. Name one of the two men who led the conspiracy to kill Caesar.

7. Who was Queen Elizabeth I's mother?

8. Name the British Admiral who defeated the Franco-Spanish fleets at Trafalgar. If you squint, you can see his statue all the way atop the monument at Trafalgar Square.

9. What great Chinese Ming explorer went to Western Asia, Southeast Asia, and even the Middle East? He did all of this more than 50 years before Columbus.

10. Which philosopher wrote *The Prince*, explaining how a harsh leader can maintain power?

Answer Sheet

Historical People
3 Rolls

Name_____

1.	
2.	
3.	
4.	
5.	
6.	
7.	
8.	
9.	
10.	

Answer Sheet

Historical People
3 Rolls

Name_____

1.	
2.	
3.	
4.	
5.	
6.	
7.	
8.	
9.	
10.	

Answer Sheet

Historical People
3 Rolls

Name_____

1.	
2.	
3.	
4.	
5.	
6.	
7.	
8.	
9.	
10.	

After you have filled out the sheet, fold your column underneath along the dashed line so the next restroom user won't see your answers. *The first player uses the far right column.*

Notes:

Notes:

Notes:

History After 1800

 One Roll

 Flip to pg. 92 for answers

1. What did Russia sell to the United States in 1867 for $7,200,000? With gas prices as they are, this wasn't such a bad deal in hindsight.

2. Which American President received the Nobel Peace Prize before completing his first year in office?

3. What was the name of the hysteria concerning computers not working once the calendar read 1/1/2000?

4. What vehicle was fitted with bulletproof glass after an assassination attempt on Pope John Paul II in 1981?

5. What country did Mustafa Kemal Atatürk become the first president of? Sound it out.

6. What did Nikita Khrushchev do at the United Nations after a delegate from the Philippines said that the USSR had swallowed up Eastern Europe?

7. Which Einstein theory stated that space and time can change when measured against an object travelling at the speed of light?

8. "One small step for man, one giant leap for mankind," were the first words said from where?

9. What crop that failed in Ireland led to extreme emigration in the 1840s?

10. What were the two Japanese cities virtually destroyed by atomic bombs in 1945?

Answer Sheet

History After 1800
1 Roll

Name_____

Answer Sheet

History After 1800
1 Roll

Name_____

Answer Sheet

History After 1800
1 Roll

Name_____

1.	1.	1.
2.	2.	2.
3.	3.	3.
4.	4.	4.
5.	5.	5.
6.	6.	6.
7.	7.	7.
8.	8.	8.
9.	9.	9.
10.	10.	10.

After you have filled out the sheet, fold your column underneath along the dashed line so the next restroom user won't see your answers. *The first player uses the far right column.*

Notes: *Notes:*   *Notes:*

History After 1800

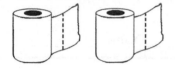

Two Rolls

Flip to pg. 93 for answers

1. What project of Czar Nicholas II became the largest railway in the world?

2. What 1883 volcanic eruption released more energy than thousands of atomic bombs? The eruption was even felt in Australia.

3. What is the name of the "lightning war" used by the Nazis in WWII?

4. What is the term given to the massacre of peaceful Russian protesters in 1905? A day of the week is in the answer.

5. On what city did 277,000 planes drop aid in 1948?

6. What country, founded by the British as a penal colony for convicts, later boomed with immigration because of cheap land offerings after 1800?

7. How many points for peace did Woodrow Wilson have?

8. Name one of the two islands that Napoleon was banished to.

9. Yasir Arafat was the leader of the PLO. What does PLO stand for?

10. Do you *remember* where Davy Crockett was killed?

Answer Sheet

History After 1800
2 Rolls

Name_____

Answer Sheet

History After 1800
2 Rolls

Name_____

Answer Shee

History After 1800
2 Rolls

Name_____

1.	1.	1.
2.	2.	2.
3.	3.	3.
4.	4.	4.
5.	5.	5.
6.	6.	6.
7.	7.	7.
8.	8.	8.
9.	9.	9.
10.	10.	10.

After you have filled out the sheet, fold your column underneath along the dashed line so the next restroom user won't see your answers. *The first player uses the far right column.*

Notes: *Notes:*   *Notes:*

History After 1800

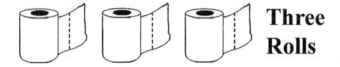

Three Rolls

Flip to pg. 94 for answers

1. From what culture in history did Adolf Hitler take the hooked cross, or swastika?

2. What was the name of the 1989 revolution in Czechoslovakia that ended Communist control? It was very soft and fuzzy.

3. Did you see the movie *The Last Emperor*? We hope so. Name the last dynasty, or the last Emperor of China? Yes, it's the boy.

4. Which European leader's private parts somehow wound up in New Jersey?

5. What American Secretary of State was responsible for the Open Door Policy with China?

6. What was Manfred von Richthofen better known as?

7. Today, Alfred Nobel is remembered for his charitable prize. However, when his obituary came out while he was still alive, he was only remembered for inventing what?

8. Which 1928 pact condemned war, and any use of war other than self-defense? Sounds like a cereal company.

9. Who led the 1804 slave revolt in Haiti? His last name was French for "opening."

10. On June 4, 1989, where did the world see "Tank Man"?

Answer Sheet

History After 1800
3 Rolls

Name_____

Answer Sheet

History After 1800
3 Rolls

Name_____

Answer Sheet

History After 1800
3 Rolls

Name_____

1.	1.	1.
2.	2.	2.
3.	3.	3.
4.	4.	4.
5.	5.	5.
6.	6.	6.
7.	7.	7.
8.	8.	8.
9.	9.	9.
10.	10.	10.

After you have filled out the sheet, fold your column underneath along the dashed line so the next restroom user won't see your answers. ***The first player uses the far right column.***

Notes:

Notes:

Notes:

World Geography

One Roll

Flip to pg. 95 for answers

1. What is the smallest ocean in the world?

2. What continent has more than half of the world's population?

3. What imaginary line goes right through Greenwich, England?

4. If you are standing on the equator, and want to go to the Tropic of Cancer, in which direction do you walk?

5. What is the longest river in the world?

6. In what mountain range would one find Mount Everest?

7. What island off the East Coast of Africa is also the name of a computer-animated movie about zoo animals?

8. According to the Richter Scale which measures earthquakes, what number has to be registered for an earthquake to be considered "massive," or "super?" Thankfully, this has never happened in the modern era.

9. Which desert is nearly as large as the United States or Europe?

10. Which country gets its name from 0 degrees latitude?

Answer Sheet

World Geography
1 Roll

Name_____

Answer Sheet

World Geography
1 Roll

Name_____

Answer Sheet

World Geography
1 Roll

Name_____

1.	1.	1.
2.	2.	2.
3.	3.	3.
4.	4.	4.
5.	5.	5.
6.	6.	6.
7.	7.	7.
8.	8.	8.
9.	9.	9.
10.	10.	10.

After you have filled out the sheet, fold your column underneath along the dashed line so the next restroom user won't see your answers. *The first player uses the far right column.*

Notes: *Notes:*   *Notes:*

World Geography

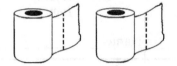

Two Rolls

Flip to pg. 96 for answers

1. In what country would you be standing to-day if you were in ancient Mesopotamia?

2. What country has the most time zones?

3. Name two of the three countries on the Iberian Peninsula.

4. What sea would one have to cross to go from Greece to Turkey?

5. What two countries in Africa start with the letter "Z?"

6. Name one of the two countries closest to Antarctica.

7. What connects the Red Sea to the Mediterranean Sea?

8. What capital of the Philippines is the most densely populated city in the world?

9. What is the most widely spoken language in the world?

10. The shoreline of what inland body of water is the lowest dry land elevation on Earth?

Answer Sheet

World Geography
2 Rolls

Name_____

Answer Sheet

World Geography
2 Rolls

Name_____

Answer Sheet

World Geography
2 Rolls

Name_____

1.	1.	1.
2.	2.	2.
3.	3.	3.
4.	4.	4.
5.	5.	5.
6.	6.	6.
7.	7.	7.
8.	8.	8.
9.	9.	9.
10.	10.	10.

After you have filled out the sheet, fold your column underneath along the dashed line so the next restroom user won't see your answers. *The first player uses the far right column.*

Notes: | *Notes:* | *Notes:*

World Geography

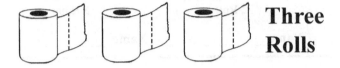

Three Rolls

Flip to pg. 97 for answers

1. Historically, where in Russia could you have lived in three different cities without ever moving?

2. What is the nickname of the area of the world that has an enormous amount of earthquakes and volcanic eruptions? If you don't know, maybe Johnny Cash can help you out.

3. What famous lake of Incan lore is now the highest commercially navigated lake on Earth?

4. What were the two previous names of the city of Istanbul?

5. What is the world's largest hydroelectric project? When it was built, it displaced thousands of people who lived along the Yangtze River.

6. How many Canadian provinces are there?

7. You might be surprised to know that this country has the world's largest per capita crime rate.

8. If you were in Kolkata (Calcutta), and were tired of swimming in the Ganges River, what nearby bay might you travel to for a dip?

9. Within ten, how many countries are there in the world?

10. Name two countries that are in *both* Europe and Asia.

Answer Sheet

World Geography
3 Rolls

Name_____

1.
2.
3.
4.
5.
6.
7.
8.
9.
10.

Answer Sheet

World Geography
3 Rolls

Name_____

1.
2.
3.
4.
5.
6.
7.
8.
9.
10.

Answer Sheet

World Geography
3 Rolls

Name_____

1.
2.
3.
4.
5.
6.
7.
8.
9.
10.

After you have filled out the sheet, fold your column underneath along the dashed line so the next restroom user won't see your answers. *The first player uses the far right column.*

Notes: *Notes:*   *Notes:*

Rulers

 ## One Roll — Answers

1. Montezuma

2. Golda Meir

3. Ivan the Terrible

4. Mohandas K. Gandhi

5. Mao Zedong (Mao Tse Tung)

6. Joan of Arc

7. Alexander the Great

8. Archduke Franz Ferdinand

9. Napoleon

10. King Hammurabi

Rulers

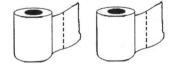 **Two Rolls — Answers**

1. Louis XIV

2. Genghis Khan

3. Vladimir Lenin. A team of doctors work around the clock to make sure that he doesn't decompose. In recent years, this has become an intensifying struggle.

4. Pharaoh Khufu

5. Marie Antoinette

6. Winston Churchill

7. Hadrian

8. Franklin Delano Roosevelt

9. Simón Bolivar

10. Francisco Franco

Rulers

 **Three Rolls —
Answers**

1. Justinian I

2. William Henry Harrison

3. Romanov. So too, it was the family name of the future czars. Even Nicholas II's children, including Anastasia, had the name Romanov.

4. Shah Jahan. He wanted the building to honor the memory of his wife, Mumtaz Mahal.

5. Hatshepsut

6. Otto von Bismarck

7. Pericles

8. Frederick the Great

9. Neville Chamberlain

10. Haile Selassie

Wars

 One Roll — Answers

1. Waterloo

2. D-Day - June 6, 1944

3. Hundred Years' War

4. The Civil War

5. The Cuban Missile Crisis

6. The Crusades

7. WWI. *Time Magazine* claims to have used the term WWI in 1939, making them the first publication to do so.

8. Charles de Gaulle

9. *Enola Gay*

10. Sticks and stones...for everyone would have already died in WWIII

Wars

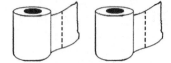 ## Two Rolls — Answers

1. *Tora! Tora! Tora!*

2. Hannibal

3. Dien Bien Phu

4. Mao Zedong (Mao Tse Tung)

5. The *Lusitania*

6. The Peloponnesian War

7. Wars of the Roses

8. The French and Indian War

9. 38th parallel

10. Leon Trotsky

Wars

Three Rolls —
Answers

1. The Thirty Years War. The Catholics were unhurt because they landed in a huge pile of manure.

2. Battle of the Bulge

3. Crimean War

4. Glorious Revolution

5. Gavrilo Princip

6. The Sepoy Rebellion (Sepoy Mutiny). Both Hindu and Muslim Indian soldiers did not take kindly to rumors of meat-flavored gunpowder packets. Such meat would violate their religious beliefs.

7. The War of Jenkins' Ear. The ear of British captain Robert Jenkins was severed by a Spanish officer in 1731. He presented it to Parliament, and they were all ears.

8. Only 22. Of the 22, 11 were given the death penalty. Thousands of Nazis escaped prosecution.

9. The Russo-Japanese War. A frustrated Theodore Roosevelt presided, and blamed both sides for causing his hair to go gray. For his efforts, he was rewarded in 1906 by becoming the first American to receive the Nobel Peace Prize.

10. The Boer Wars

World Landmarks

 ## One Roll — Answers

1. The Great Wall of China. It has over 10,000 watchtowers. Contrary to popular myth, you can not see it from outer space.

2. The Great Pyramid of Giza

3. Westminster Abbey

4. Normandy. If you said Bayeux, that's good, too. Bayeux is home to the Bayeux tapestry, the largest in the world. It depicts the story of the Norman Conquest, and even has a picture of Haley's Comet embroidered into it.

5. Versailles

6. Rio de Janeiro, Brazil

7. Stonehenge. It's not the largest ancient collection of stones, but it has become the most famous. No one's positive what it is. Odds are it's a calendar to mark the winter solstice.

8. The Bastille. Today a monument marks where it used to stand in Paris. For the remains of the Bastille, you have to travel about a half-mile away to a small park visited by few tourists.

9. The Wailing Wall, or Western Wall

10. The Eiffel Tower. It's true. Many were opposed to it being built. Today, it's one of the most recognizable structures in the world.

World Landmarks

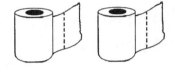

Two Rolls — Answers

1. Machu Picchu

2. The Washington Monument. Construction began in 1848, but a lack of funding, political disagreements, and the Civil War left it unfinished until 1884.

3. Pearl Harbor. Today, the oil from the ship is still visible on the surface of the water.

4. Chichen Itza

5. Tiananmen Square. It's supposed to hold one million people.

6. Agra, India

7. Athena

8. The Leaning Tower of Pisa. Experts say that the tower leans about a millimeter more each year.

9. Nazca, Peru. Monkeys, insects, and random patterns mark this deserted, mysterious area.

10. St. Basil's Cathedral, or Cathedral of St. Vasily the Blessed. Everyone's seen it, but not everyone can remember its name.

World Landmarks

Three Rolls — Answers

1. There are several replicas of the Statue of Liberty. But, the one directly related to her is in Paris. It's the life-sized cast that stands tall in Luxembourg Gardens. It's actually facing and saluting the one in New York.

2. La Galerie des Glaces, or the Hall of Mirrors, at the Palace of Versailles

3. Crete

4. The Hague

5. Angkor Wat

6. The Forbidden City. If you slept in a different room every day of your life, it would take you until age 27 before you slept in the same room twice.

7. Hagia Sophia

8. Petra

9. Sanctuary of Apollo at Delphi

10. La Sagrada Familia. Gaudi's cathedral has taken over 100 years to complete. He once said, "My client is not in a hurry." The project is scheduled to be completed in 2026.

History Before 1800

 ## One Roll — Answers

1. The Triangular Trade

2. China. It was used for fireworks, and then explosives.

3. The bubonic plague, or the Black Death

4. Leif Ericson

5. Hieroglyphics

6. Elizabeth I...she never married

7. The Guillotine, invented by Doctor Joseph Ignac Guillotin (no "e" at the end of his name). His machine would be the spectacle of the French Revolution. It was said that even women would wear guillotine earrings to a public execution.

8. **Protest**ant...if you never realized that, you just got your money's worth

9. The Terracotta Army. It was one of the greatest archaeological finds in world history. What was the reward for the farmers who found it? Not much...some grain, and eventually a low-paying job signing autographs at the tourist site.

10. The Ottoman Empire

History Before 1800

 **Two Rolls — Answers**

1. Mount Vesuvius. That's the volcano that covered and preserved ancient Pompeii.

2. Catherine the Great. It's one of those unsubstantiated rumors that was probably started by her adversaries. Sadly, it's one of the first things that come to historians' minds when hearing her name.

3. The Silk Roads

4. *Coup d'état*

5. Globe Theatre

6. A tennis court

7. Samurai warrior

8. King Solomon

9. Romulus and Remus

10. Habeas Corpus Act

History Before 1800

Three Rolls — Answers

1. Six. Catherine of Aragon (divorced), Anne Boleyn (beheaded), Jane Seymour (died), Anne of Cleves (divorced), Kathryn Howard (beheaded), Katherine Parr (survived). Everyone together now! That's *divorced, beheaded, died, divorced, beheaded, survived.*

2. Nebuchadnezzar. A Nebuchadnezzar can hold 20 standard bottles of wine.

3. *The Epic of Gilgamesh*

4. Peace of Westphalia

5. Don Quixote. It is considered by many to be a landmark work in both Spanish, and Western literature.

6. Vlad the Impaler, or Vlad III. Though he wasn't suspected of being a vampire, he did impale a lot of skulls on spikes to intimidate his enemies.

7. Ramses II

8. Charles I

9. Phoenicians

10. Ur

Popular Culture

 One Roll — Answers

1. Luciano Pavarotti

2. Oliver Twist

3. It's the *Flamenco*, not the Flamingo!

4. Vincent van Gogh. It probably wasn't his entire ear, but his ear lobe. There's even a case that van Gogh didn't do this himself, and it was either accidentally or purposely cut off by his friend in a fight. That friend was artist, and fencer, Paul Gauguin.

5. *...Bollywood."*

6. Ludwig van Beethoven

7. The Beatles

8. Sydney Opera House

9. Roman Colosseum

10. Basketball. James Naismith used peach baskets and soccer balls.

Popular Culture

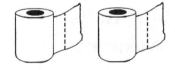 ## Two Rolls — Answers

1. Amsterdam. Yes, that information center really does exist.

2. Pamplona, Spain

3. Haiku

4. Naples

5. Rembrandt

6. Columbia Broadcasting System

7. Pink Floyd

8. Athens

9. *Oedipus Rex*, hence the Oedipus complex

10. Strawberries and cream

Popular Culture

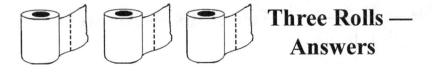

Three Rolls — Answers

1. Avenue des Champs-Élysées

2. Kabuki Theater

3. They throw them at each other! The event is called La Tomatina, and it is held on the last Wednesday of August. It's usually on the news every year, and is followed up by some type of witty comment from the anchorperson.

4. *Othello*

5. The Spanish Riding School in Vienna. Yes, they choreograph horse dancing.

6. Ceviche

7. Auguste Rodin

8. The Roman Circus. The largest outdoor stadium in ancient Rome was the Circus Maximus

9. Troubadours

10. The Czech Republic…yes, they beat the Germans

Religion and Philosophy

 ## One Roll — Answers

1. Mount Sinai

2. Hinduism

3. The Sistine Chapel

4. Islam

5. Plato

6. Christianity

7. Martin Luther

8. The Koran (Qur'an)

9. Exodus

10. Zeus

Religion and Philosophy

 **Two Rolls — Answers**

1. Ka'ba

2. Shinto

3. Bhagavad Gita

4. Roman Catholicism

5. Blood

6. Confucius

7. Nirvana

8. Atheism

9. The Egyptian Book of the Dead. Many believe the text's name was the inspiration behind the name of the band, The Grateful Dead.

10. The pilgrimage to Mecca that all Muslims must make

Religion and Philosophy

 **Three Rolls — Answers**

1. Siddhartha Gautama

2. Vishnu

3. Tao Te Ching

4. Isis

5. The sun

6. Buddhism

7. Pluto

8. Kabbalah

9. Jainism

10. I Ching

Dates (Get within 5 years either way)

 ## One Roll — Answers

1. 1941

2. 1789

3. 1492

4. 1969

5. 2011

6. 1919

7. 1929

8. 1917

9. 1944

10. 2012

Dates (Get within 5 years either way)

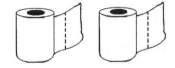 **Two Rolls — Answers**

1. 1066

2. 1588

3. 1989

4. 1947

5. 44 BC

6. 1981

7. 1949

8. 1967

9. 1945

10. 1215

Dates (Get within 5 years either way)

Three Rolls — Answers

1. 1853

2. 1804

3. 476 AD

4. 399 BC

5. 1814-1815

6. 1870-1871

7. 800

8. 1803

9. 1848

10. 1900

Historical People

 One Roll — Answers

1. Homer

2. Leonardo da Vinci

3. Nelson Mandela. He then, of course, became President of South Africa.

4. Michelangelo

5. Orville and Wilbur

6. Marco Polo

7. Mother Teresa

8. Sigmund Freud

9. Marie Curie

10. Charles Lindbergh

Historical People

Two Rolls — Answers

1. Michelangelo

2. Raphael

3. Friedrich Engels

4. Charles Darwin. Darwin's observations were mostly made in the Galápagos Islands. His theory of evolution creates debate even today.

5. The printing press

6. Ferdinand Magellan

7. Jonas Salk

8. King Tutankhamun (King Tut). His name is quite famous because of the tomb, but his father, Akhenaten, is a much bigger name among Egyptologists.

9. Robert Fulton. He is buried in New York City at Trinity Church, right next to Alexander Hamilton. You can see both graves from the street.

10. Mary Shelley. Remember, Frankenstein is the doctor...not the monster! If you dressed up like Frankenstein for Halloween, you would be wearing a stethoscope.

Historical People

Three Rolls — Answers

1. Ivan Pavlov

2. Voltaire

3. William Wallace

4. Klemens von Metternich. Metternich wanted to maintain a balance of power, and restore monarchs dethroned by Napoleon.

5. *The Art of War*

6. Gaius Cassius and Marcus Brutus. Caesar was stabbed 23 times.

7. Anne Boleyn. The same Anne Boleyn who was executed by Henry VIII.

8. Horatio Nelson

9. Zheng He. Some believe he is the greatest explorer of all time. His fleets of ships dwarfed what Europe would send out decades later. For uncertain reasons, the Ming government ended the voyages. Who knows…had they not, the New World could have been discovered by a Chinese explorer.

10. Niccolò Machiavelli

History After 1800

 ## One Roll — Answers

1. Alaska. That's 2 cents per acre. Obviously, a way better deal than the Louisiana Purchase which was 3 cents per acre. Secretary of State William Seward was ridiculed for this purchase at the time, as the deal was nicknamed "Seward's Folly."

2. Barack Obama

3. Y2K

4. The Popemobile

5. Turkey

6. He banged his shoe on the desk

7. Theory of Relativity

8. The Moon. Neil Armstrong has been criticized for bad grammar, but he contends that he said "One small step for [a] man, one giant leap for mankind."

9. The potato

10. "Little Boy" was dropped on Hiroshima by the *Enola Gay* on Aug. 6th, and "Fat Man" was dropped by *Bockscar* on Nagasaki on Aug. 9th

History After 1800

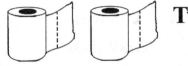 **Two Rolls — Answers**

1. Trans-Siberian Railway

2. Krakatoa

3. Blitzkrieg

4. Bloody Sunday

5. Berlin. The Berlin Airlift was one of many instances during the Cold War where another World War could have ignited. At the peak of Allied flights, there was a plane dropping aid every 30 seconds to the people of Berlin.

6. Australia

7. Fourteen. His 14th point was to call for a general association of nations, or the League of Nations. After WWI, the United States would not join because of a fear of losing its neutrality.

8. Elba and St. Helena

9. Palestine Liberation Organization

10. The Alamo

History After 1800

Three Rolls — Answers

1. Indian. It was used in Hinduism, Buddhism, and Jainism way earlier than it was in Germany. The word is a Sanskrit term.

2. Velvet Revolution

3. Qing or Manchu Dynasty. Pu Yi or Henry Pu Yi.

4. Napoleon. According to legend, and doubted by some, it was cut off during his last rites, and bought and sold throughout Europe. Most recently it was purchased in 1969 by New Jersey urologist Dr. John K. Lattimer for about $40,000. The doctor has since passed, and the organ now belongs to his daughter.

5. John Hay

6. The Red Baron. Richthofen scored over 80 victories, and is considered one of the greatest aces in air-combat history. He was killed in the final months of WWI.

7. Dynamite. When Alfred's brother died, a French newspaper published the wrong obituary. It was of Alfred! They castigated him for such a destructive invention. Afterward, he came up with a better way to be remembered.

8. Kellogg-Briand Pact. WWII would start about a decade later.

9. Toussaint L' Ouverture

10. A protester stood in front of an approaching tank at the Tiananmen Square Massacre in Beijing. It was caught on tape, and shared around the world. There is no certain identification of who Tank Man was, though there are some rumors and theories.

World Geography

One Roll — Answers

1. The Arctic Ocean

2. Asia. If you think Manhattan is congested, try Beijing!

3. The Prime Meridian

4. North

5. Nile. Some scientists believe that the Amazon is longer. It depends on how you measure. If you said either river, give yourself the point.

6. The Himalayas

7. Madagascar

8. Ten. A 10.0 earthquake would be 10x stronger than a 9.0, or "Great," earthquake. A 9.0 was about the power of the 2011 Japanese earthquake, and the 2004 one that caused the Indian Ocean tsunami.

9. The Sahara Desert

10. Ecuador

World Geography

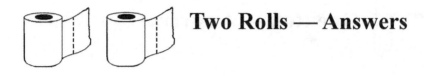

Two Rolls — Answers

1. Iraq

2. Russia. They have decreased their time zones in recent years. Presently there are 9.

3. Spain, Portugal, and Andorra

4. The Aegean Sea

5. Zambia and Zimbabwe

6. Chile and Argentina

7. Suez Canal

8. At 38.55 square km, and over 16 million people, Manila is the most densely populated city in the world.

9. Mandarin Chinese

10. The Dead Sea

World Geography

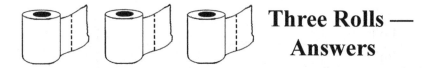

Three Rolls — Answers

1. St. Petersburg. You could have been born in St. Petersburg, raised in Petrograd, and died in Leningrad. All three are the same place. "Burg" sounded too German during WWI, so it became "Petrograd" in 1914. Then when Lenin died in 1924, it became Leningrad. Of course, if you lived to be about 80, you would have seen the city return to the same one you were born in, St Petersburg (1991).

2. The Ring of Fire

3. Lake Titicaca

4. It was Byzantium, then Constantinople, and now Istanbul

5. Three Gorges Dam

6. Ten. Alberta, British Columbia, Manitoba, New Brunswick, Newfoundland, Nova Scotia, Ontario, Prince Edward Island, Quebec, Saskatchewan. There are also three territories.

7. Vatican City. With all of the tourists funneling into such a small area, there is a massive amount of pick-pocketing.

8. Bay of Bengal

9. Though a fluctuating number, there is a consensus that 196 countries exist in the world as of August, 2011. This could have changed by the time you read this. Hence, give yourself a leeway of ten.

10. Azerbaijan, Georgia, Kazakhstan, Russia, Turkey. Some consider Armenia to be in both as well, but the UN classifies it as Asia. If you said Armenia, count it.

Scorecard — Name: _____

Category	# Right		# of Pts.		Tot. Pts.
Rulers - 1 Roll		x	1	=	
Rulers - 2 Rolls		x	2	=	
Rulers - 3 Rolls		x	3	=	
Wars - 1 Roll		x	1	=	
Wars - 2 Rolls		x	2	=	
Wars - 3 Rolls		x	3	=	
World Landmarks - 1 Roll		x	1	=	
World Landmarks - 2 Rolls		x	2	=	
World Landmarks - 3 Rolls		x	3	=	
History Before 1800 - 1 Roll		x	1	=	
History Before 1800 - 2 Rolls		x	2	=	
History Before 1800 - 3 Rolls		x	3	=	
Popular Culture - 1 Roll		x	1	=	
Popular Culture - 2 Rolls		x	2	=	
Popular Culture - 3 Rolls		x	3	=	
Religion and Philosophy - 1 Roll		x	1	=	
Religion and Philosophy - 2 Rolls		x	2	=	
Religion and Philosophy - 3 Rolls		x	3	=	
Dates - 1 Roll		x	1	=	
Dates - 2 Rolls		x	2	=	
Dates - 3 Rolls		x	3	=	
Historical People - 1 Roll		x	1	=	
Historical People - 2 Rolls		x	2	=	
Historical People - 3 Rolls		x	3	=	
History After 1800 - 1 Roll		x	1	=	
History After 1800 - 2 Rolls		x	2	=	
History After 1800 - 3 Rolls		x	3	=	
World Geography - 1 Roll		x	1	=	
World Geography - 2 Rolls		x	2	=	
World Geography - 3 Rolls		x	3	=	

Grand Total

Scorecard — Name: _____

Category	# Right		# of Pts.		Tot. Pts.
Rulers - 1 Roll		x	1	=	
Rulers - 2 Rolls		x	2	=	
Rulers - 3 Rolls		x	3	=	
Wars - 1 Roll		x	1	=	
Wars - 2 Rolls		x	2	=	
Wars - 3 Rolls		x	3	=	
World Landmarks - 1 Roll		x	1	=	
World Landmarks - 2 Rolls		x	2	=	
World Landmarks - 3 Rolls		x	3	=	
History Before 1800 - 1 Roll		x	1	=	
History Before 1800 - 2 Rolls		x	2	=	
History Before 1800 - 3 Rolls		x	3	=	
Popular Culture - 1 Roll		x	1	=	
Popular Culture - 2 Rolls		x	2	=	
Popular Culture - 3 Rolls		x	3	=	
Religion and Philosophy - 1 Roll		x	1	=	
Religion and Philosophy - 2 Rolls		x	2	=	
Religion and Philosophy - 3 Rolls		x	3	=	
Dates - 1 Roll		x	1	=	
Dates - 2 Rolls		x	2	=	
Dates - 3 Rolls		x	3	=	
Historical People - 1 Roll		x	1	=	
Historical People - 2 Rolls		x	2	=	
Historical People - 3 Rolls		x	3	=	
History After 1800 - 1 Roll		x	1	=	
History After 1800 - 2 Rolls		x	2	=	
History After 1800 - 3 Rolls		x	3	=	
World Geography - 1 Roll		x	1	=	
World Geography - 2 Rolls		x	2	=	
World Geography - 3 Rolls		x	3	=	

Grand Total

Scorecard — Name: _____

Category	# Right		# of Pts.		Tot. Pts.
Rulers - 1 Roll		x	1	=	
Rulers - 2 Rolls		x	2	=	
Rulers - 3 Rolls		x	3	=	
Wars - 1 Roll		x	1	=	
Wars - 2 Rolls		x	2	=	
Wars - 3 Rolls		x	3	=	
World Landmarks - 1 Roll		x	1	=	
World Landmarks - 2 Rolls		x	2	=	
World Landmarks - 3 Rolls		x	3	=	
History Before 1800 - 1 Roll		x	1	=	
History Before 1800 - 2 Rolls		x	2	=	
History Before 1800 - 3 Rolls		x	3	=	
Popular Culture - 1 Roll		x	1	=	
Popular Culture - 2 Rolls		x	2	=	
Popular Culture - 3 Rolls		x	3	=	
Religion and Philosophy - 1 Roll		x	1	=	
Religion and Philosophy - 2 Rolls		x	2	=	
Religion and Philosophy - 3 Rolls		x	3	=	
Dates - 1 Roll		x	1	=	
Dates - 2 Rolls		x	2	=	
Dates - 3 Rolls		x	3	=	
Historical People - 1 Roll		x	1	=	
Historical People - 2 Rolls		x	2	=	
Historical People - 3 Rolls		x	3	=	
History After 1800 - 1 Roll		x	1	=	
History After 1800 - 2 Rolls		x	2	=	
History After 1800 - 3 Rolls		x	3	=	
World Geography - 1 Roll		x	1	=	
World Geography - 2 Rolls		x	2	=	
World Geography - 3 Rolls		x	3	=	

Grand Total

How did you do?

500 + — King/Queen of the Throne

400-499 — Topper of the Hopper

350-399 — Porcelain Prince/Princess

300-349 — Toileterrific!

250-299 — Keep Flushing for the Stars

200-249 — Might Need a Plunger

150-199 — Gotta call the Plumber

Below 150 — Clogged

Try a different Toiletrivia Book!

Made in the USA
Middletown, DE
09 December 2023